Damage

JACQUE VAUGHT BROGAN

University of Notre Dame Press
Notre Dame, Indiana

Published by the University of Notre Dame Press
Notre Dame, Indiana 46556
www.undpress.nd.edu

Manufactured in the United States of America

Library of Congress Cataloging-in-Publication Data
Brogan, Jacqueline Vaught, 1952–
Damage / Jacque Vaught Brogan.
p.   cm.
ISBN 0-268-02560-6 (cloth : alk. paper)
ISBN 0-268-02561-4 (pbk. : alk. paper)
I. Title.
PS3602.R637 D36   2003
811'.54—dc21

                    2003004345

∞ *This book is printed on acid-free paper.*

CONTENTS

Acknowledgments   vii

Windows

It's Like This—   3
A Voice from a High-Rise   5
Five O'Clock News   7
Cancellations   8
Window   10
Pain Happens   11
To the Leaves and All—   13
Before the Fire   14
Fire Pine   16
Walking into Blue Waters   17

Blue Waters

Stable   21
Wellesley   22
Damage   23
Sometimes   24
Friday Nights   25
Anniversary   26
Leavings   27
Gemini   28
The Bond   29
The Turning   30

Notes from the Body

i. "(T)here's a world" — 33

ii. (For Sandra) — 34

vi. (Color Report) — 36

viii. Eytmology 1816—
      Naming the 19th State *Indiana* — 38

ix. Fire Spirit — 40

xiv. Notes from the Body— — 41

xxii. "Tonight both of my hands are cold" — 44

xxiii. Solstice — 46

xxix. All the Unravelings — 47

xxxii. Underneath All the Fabrications — 48

Notes from the Body: — 50

ACKNOWLEDGMENTS

Grateful acknowledgment is made to editors of the journals in which several of these poems have appeared previously, though at times in very different forms:

Anthology of New England Writers
"The Bond"

Bitterroot
"Walking into Blue Waters"

Connecticut Poetry Review
"Sometimes"

Connotations
"NOTES FROM THE BODY"

Hubbub
"Window "

Kalliope
"Friday Nights," "Notes from the Body"

Poetry International
"It's Like This—," selections from "Notes from the Body"

Spring: The E. E. Cummings Journal
"Stable," "Damage," selections from "Notes from the Body"

Trinity Review
"Wellesley"

Wallace Stevens Journal
" A Voice from a High-Rise," "Fire Pine," "Before the Fire"

Windows

IT'S LIKE THIS—

Frigates come close, children run
right in to the water,

feel exquisitely the sand
shifting under toe,

arms gesturing almost like words in the sun.
Farther off shore

waves build in deepening crescendoes, yellow
tangs drift,

simultaneously, in and out of stone-
flowered corals.

On land, light strokes a mother's skin
like a forgotten

lover, as if with surprise palm trees wave in
rooted pleasure,

even as two boys, perhaps seniors at Iolani,
catch the one, great

breaker, stand tensed, like odd dancers,
feet placed just so,

their arms exclaiming this triumphant motion—
Later, when

the ambulance and fire engine come
and people run down

to the Point like excited birds to see
the exact spot

that already bears no stain of where one skull
cracked on the rocks,

the ocean goes on, as if from a distance,
offering wave after wave,

—with their many flashing coins—and no hope
or desire or pardon.

A VOICE FROM A HIGH-RISE

In 1941, he explained it—
the pressure of reality, violence
of a war-like whole, news of Asia,

Africa, Europe—all at one time—at
exclusion of the mind, a violence
against the spirit, for everyone alive.

I've learned it, and I've seen it—
the mother who heard from a microphone
her son's continuing cry, as

he fell away from the mountain,
another who listened to her small
child, by radio, as he choked

in the deepening mud of a mine,
the picture of the four-year-old
girl, suffocated, even as her parents spoke

to guests brought into their home,
the pleas, for help, of the twelve-year-old,
heard for days after the Mexican quake,

on television, carried by satellite
to us in Honolulu, while no crane
could raise the rubble from him in time.

I hope you fare better—are all right—
though it's more these times than
I can bear. It's more than enough here—the wife

dismembered, head dropped in the waters
off Waipahu, hands stuck at an angle in a trash can,
and the street people, just beyond my lights.

FIVE O'CLOCK NEWS

"More on the war against writing on the walls . . ."

"We won't have it, the latest thing
gangs are doing. Instead of being
in the streets fighting, they're racing

> Defining Yosemite, glaciers left
> deep marks, a literal alphabet
> too large to see, so John Muir called it,

"all over town, trying to out-do
each other with their artwork. You
see how quickly I wrote **this,** *with a blue*

> that recorded the earth's own conquests
> and defeats, whole mountains by ice
> subdued, like some girls' eyes.

"broad-tipped felt marker? Now minors
must give addresses and phone numbers
(and we keep the markers behind counters)."

> This is a script we would not erase,
> however violent, from the granite face,
> positioning, as it does, this human place.

CANCELLATIONS

Fifteen years ago—an aberrant scene,
it seemed, played and played again
as if we needed prompting

to memorize the lines
the grotesque swan of the clouds
etched in air and left lingering there

("Gruesome Beauty," the newspapers
called the white arc of the exploding
evaporating Challenger)

as if never reaching back to water.
—We all stopped,
as though every wave

were suddenly capped with doubt,
felt for ourselves this important failure—
a sudden shuddering inside,

the shuttle gone, yet still
bearing names we all learned
including one, Onizuka,

from our islands. But now
(as if escalated beyond comprehension,
apocalyptic implosions,

the sudden rain of bodies and burning air),
we watch this scene
over and over, as if caught in an act

we can never describe:
the eerie silence of the skies,
all flights cancelled,

an oddly blank, innocent blue above
that can never register all the names,
or even who, or quite what, to blame.

WINDOW

I have known something of terror,
and seen the bodies where
the chisel of long starvation

has exposed the underlying bones,
and here, the five women carved,
limb from limb, like stones.

For a long time the fear
was personal, dreams of my father
burning me in a kiln

even as my mother called me home.
Or, just looking back, finding
I have lived alone.

I haven't had to imagine
it—or you—
As if from the distance of a god,

we've seen the surprise of color
rise over the moon,
something blue, brown, and green

(with a swirling white mosaic) lift
majestically in the dark
as if something

utterly miraculous
must be being
shaped there—**Here**—

PAIN HAPPENS

In objects
where subject

cannot speak—
like rape—

like the gutting
of earth, whole stars

turned (per-verse)
into flaming flowers

fumigating
the land, over and over

before our faces—
unless—

words unleash
the blue and pink,

patterns at our feet
sheaths of wheat

and beckon, thin
birds turned

asunder, turned
aside, settling

briefly while
words lift—

spring colors
in autumn winds

—the soul
moving that

has been so
long kept still.

TO THE LEAVES AND ALL——

In the Southwest
leaves large enough to be seen
are scarce on the high desert plateau,

though mesquite
and cacti of various kinds
brag of the peculiar hardenings

necessary with so few clouds in sight.
But even higher, in the mountains
holding up the lands,

golden aspens of October
run over the ridges,
through the valleys,

like water
in a sudden rush of color
as if one spirit were waving its hand

saying, we are going to die,
leaves and all, but it is good
to have shared in this blaze,

heightened all the more,
by this nearing,
deepening blue sky.

BEFORE THE FIRE

In winter, bare limbs
of necessity
cut philosophers'
sharp angles in the sky.

It is a relief
after November's
heavy drizzle, dank
leaves turned mush and brown.

It comes, almost as
a surprise, the memory of spring,
that mud and mess should ever
be pleasing,

should ever be—or that
bodies should expose
themselves in summer
with such abandon

on the beach
(lying as still as
shells, as warm as sand),
before the first cold

proclaimer of winter
roars through—
and fires the leaves
into a frenzy

of colors—
infuriating to the mind
of winter, like
a mediterranean
dance.

FIRE PINE

Also called *the Bishop pine,*

it cannot release its seeds
(bound embryonic perhaps

forever) unless fire
melt the resin gluing

the scales closed—
like printed books

stored in libraries
with pages uncut.

Who could have thought
this logical? or that

whole stands of fire
pines sketch in relief

the sunset, like Japanese
woodcut prints?

Who could have imagined
this particular display,

life riddling such improbable
possibilities.

WALKING INTO BLUE WATERS

I have been talking for a long time
as a person exploring a cave.

Sometimes, my fingers trailing
the damp walls, I have needed you.

So I have spoken your name as if
in that speaking I could make you

appear. But always you were
out there, a name, a shadow

in the deepening shadows of this
place. Now, I call to you,

no longer to call you here,
but rather to name your absence,

and in that empty space to send
these words through,

like light pulsing through
the universe or oxygen entering

every cell. I come out now
a woman dressed in blue,

spreading her arms to blue
sky, walking into blue waters.

Blue Waters

STABLE

Here I am, the wild horse
in harness. Cold nights
of cruel roaming tamed
to needles, knitting, nagging.

Everyone must have known
how it would be,
but they wouldn't tell me,
the man with the dark eyes,

the old woman serving cake—
not even him, my handsome rider,
who trained me to trail his smell—
I thinking I was finally free

when everyone knew
that bride meant bridle.

WELLESLEY

Sometimes desire is
a tree's silhouette against
a few fainter stars.

Then no touch can steady
the trouble sliding
just under your skin.

And if your lover has left
or your hand, touching
her breast, is dead,

the trouble moves you
out to the streets. When
a man walks outside

of himself at night,
what's there to bring
him back in again?

No street, no tree,
and no idea of love
ever hid the terrible stars.

DAMAGE

If I cup this silence in my hand,
it's not to protect it
like some delicate bird.
It does not have wings to damage,
this thing, so solid and brutal.

This is rootless and disembodied,
even more than the wind,
for anything in isolation becomes round
and the secret inside whitens.

So now I hold this silence
to give to you the fact
of the strangers we've become,
the pale stone I've carried too long,
that's altered us—

rings, repeating, concentric circles,
defacing, erasing the pond.

SOMETIMES

A wave sliding back into itself
doesn't mean loneliness.
When wet feet curl against the wind
into the sand and themselves,
then waves are casual—
like the motion of breath.

Such times, the moon, the years'
bitter interchangeable cycles
make sense. Doesn't that final
loneliness take form only
to find itself again, as when
an old man closes his eyes

the last time and slides,
like a wave, into darkness?
Then, holding yourself against
the wind like a lost lover, you say
this is merely change,
indifferent and insignificant.

FRIDAY NIGHTS

Week after week the moon chisels
at the steady cedars
and small silver chips
are scattered on the blind
paling windows. How painful—

that brilliance when women loosen
their hair, spreading strand
from strand around studied, perfect

faces. Each one anoints
her body in a ritual of water
and oils as if preparing
herself to be presented
a virgin, again, worthy

of being chosen. How awful—
the expectations when none
will be touched completely

and disillusion hardens to boredom.
And yet, in a moment my lover
will break open the wine
and create a conversation,
as if it were still exciting,

the steady closing of the dark
while the moon chisels at our window
and the streetlights blink and gape.

ANNIVERSARY

I always remember my parents'
anniversary, April the 26th,
and the father I've never seen again
after the divorce, having confused
me in his madness and pain
with my mother. I don't think

he ever touched me, really,
though there's one dream in a blue
house with three stories
where I convince him to no longer
pretend being married, and another
where my lover, his hand

covering my mouth, tells the gas-
station attendant filling the car
I try to escape that *he* is my father,
taking me to a home. I am
a parent now, myself, wanting
to protect her from these wounds:

the reddening scab at sunset,
the arrows of the stars,
the cold ringed noose of the moon—
and the awful desire
he must have had to control,
since he could not prevent, the scars.

LEAVINGS

It is true—
the leaves have spun away in the dark.

He thought we had burned away
all that was written on them.

Soon, even our children
will be going, one by one.

My memories of the many Octobers
I have held our love

have been rewritten,
have fallen now like the brown dried leaves

scurrying across dead ground,
as if loss leaves no trace of having happened—

as if damage isn't a slow fire
that continues to smoulder underground.

GEMINI

We were at Sans Souci, my desiring
you to see the green
flash of the tropic sunset—
whatever optical illusion

expands at that precise moment
the sun has already disappeared.
Our visions are never the same.
Like the blind, all our lessons

have been learned in the dark.
This is a fact,
though perhaps it defines

your integrity, and mine,
and most certainly the space
for desire.

THE BOND

The needs we each speak
from some larger loneliness
gather the way the back
of leaves gather blue ash

at dusk. But where has the sky
ever touched exact? And what
answer to any need
breaks full as an egg?

Though I lose myself
like the sky trembling past
its horizon, I still spread
myself like a lotion. You want

me to cradle your need
and give it back, whole
and healthy, like a son.
How can I stay?

It's night: the leaves
droop heavy with dark.
We touch inside,
each wet black.

THE TURNING

When the blue heron returns in August
to my shallow pond to eat
and sometimes torture the goldfish
or bass (catching one with its bill
and then spitting it out
only to capture it again—

and again before swallowing it whole),
we know fall has arrived all over
and that love should feel like a harvest.
But of course the blue heron
never stays for long and leaves
in only a few days, as if to say,

This love is not what you meant,
at all—not the one gliding ever up
through air, pulling sunrise after sunset
in its thrilling wings—a bird's,
fish's, star's, poem's sudden turn
far past Canada, beyond the beyond—

Notes from the Body

i

(T)here's a world
of difference
between saying

I am the center
of the world
and ***This** is*
the center
of the world:

cold sun
concentric circles

(blood bearing moon
      baring moon
blood bearing maple
blood red
burning leaves
     passion
     fruit
placenta
blood bearing
    harvest
    moon)

.

ii

for Sandra, who is having a hysterectomy

Through our bodies—
stories we just re-member.
                    Mishawaka
name of nearest town named
of Indian princess.
                    Tapi Toppy
my own ancestor, Cherokee, we know not
the spelling of
                who still passed on
through her daughters this knowledge

            each stone is alive earth is alive

Spirit—we arrive like
            horses

            stand on our own
            so soon,

            never forgetting
                    that grass
                            is
                    milk,

                    wind is moon
                    menses
                    in the making.

I call my friend.
Against doctor's
    orders, she is
    keeping one
            ovary.

One's enough
she says, to keep
her health
    cycling.

vi

I. Color report—
       first, black

          absolutely
          without shine

          opaque, to the point of being,
          almost without texture

              (a netting that deep)

          then purple—
              a vibrant band
              moving
                      like a river
          pulsing
              exactly
              with your heart

          then the real black
                  the one that shines
          so oily it whitens
                      to the center

          where opens yellow-rose
          a color almost like dawn
          almost (if you weren't a man,
                  if this weren't contracted
                  there like a deliberated
                      muscle)

like a peach—
            or like a petal
     unfurling

II.   And if all mine
        are blue,

did you count the cerulean,
        sky blue,
        peacock blue—

the violet, the cornflower,
        the aquamarine—

the cyanine,
the saxony,
        the cobalt

the turquoise,
        the motion,
        the balm

the midnight sapphire
        that conceals
                but still
                        conveys
        the stars—

viii

ETYMOLOGY 1816—NAMING
THE 19TH STATE *INDIANA*

India: Skr. *sindhu* river, spec. the Indus
hence the region of the Indus,
      Sindh (by extension, with Greeks and Persians)
      the country east of this.
Applied to America or parts of it

Indies orig. India with the ad-
jacent islands, later called *East Indies*
      (*West Indies*, which had come to be applied
      to lands of the Western Hemisphere
      which were taken
      to be part
      of the Eastern group.)

      Spirit, and blessings, great mother
      no air for my voice in those words
not even logical

      The Council Oak did not die
      of old age. It fell apart, it ripped itself
      wide open to witness the rings it had weathered.

      She would have fed the ground again
      with her body. And I try to dance with mine.

They must be coming, gathering they are
the feet of women, in which there are other
                    rhythms, different logics,
who'll give the name back to this
we call St. Joseph River,
Notre Dame, Indiana,
New York, New World
taken to be part
of the Eastern group.

            What trees are left are talking
                    blazing they are this autumn—
                    with burning colors

            They say,
                    this is the history of a mistake
                    which they kept making
                    after the mistake was known

ix

FIRE SPIRIT

Somewhere, out there,
you are,
          scattered through the geo-
          graphy.

I need to open my eyes
carefully (full of care),

to the wind tickling the lake
          (coins of light are
                    skipping
                    on the waves)

and trembling the leaves
          (small ovations
          applauding
                    each reddened apple)

and to wait—
          wait for the soul
                    to climb out of the trees.

XIV

NOTES FROM THE BODY—

Is it over between us, before it's begun?

We talk, several times daily,
                at great cost.

          Something spiraling between
                  our vision—naked trees,
          gray light, flashing storms,
                        reddest aspens
                        of the fall

You're afraid of your job.
          I'm afraid of the world—

What tree, what sister,
              felled again
          whispered her last
          syllables this night?

                    And did anyone hear?

My neighbor, pregnant,
          and with a two-year old child
          was murdered.
Someone tried to break in
          to my house, twice in one week.
(My children were asleep—with only
          one staircase: no escape.)
I could go on.
                    I try to go on.

Listen: the air is hurting
like a person
who misused the once sacred
tobacco

Water is phlegming
like a person
with too many years
of too many medicines

If I can't say this
to you, whom I know best
of all, how can I speak
of it, of us, at all?

Today, *that* man was lonely,
on my street,
dressed in a heavy overcoat,
hiding something cheap—

and the river, St. Joseph's
only looked clean from the street

Children are dying
at 74 degrees heat
from hypothermia (starvation)
a whole continent is dying
(global warming) Antarctica

And we've all lost our names.
And the map stays the same—
        it says,

In every war
> *someone always rapes a corpse,*
> *someone pisses in a flagging*
> > *mouth*
> *someone puts out a cigarette*
> > *in a frozen eye*
> *someone always cuts out a tongue*
> > *not knowing why*

Is it over between us,
before it's begun?

I never bore your children
> nor danced in the sun-
> > light upon the waters
Austin, Oahu, wherever—

> this spiral, this spiro-
> > graph, even spies of my own

> keep nudging me, saying
> > *separate*
> and not because I've quit loving you—
> > aspen smells
> > flannel voice
> > leathered whispers
> > silk and skin—

> but because I'm becoming afraid
> of just how much
> I really am
> > learning
> > to hate

xxii

Tonight both of my hands are cold—
and not just from the weather

but from efforts
and letters expended
and disregarded.

And the house I've tried
for years to make my home
is cold—

the whole state is cold
an ironic symptom
of global warming
also disregarded

—while in this town,
this year alone,
random violence has already
killed three children

—a fact also somewhat disregarded.

Though my skin still sings
          to your touch,

though open desert spaces
full of light

come back to me
with just the sight
of the slight offbeat
way you walk,
it's nothing poetic,
these stiff hands,
these shifts in climate,

nor how we've finally quit talking.

xxiii

SOLSTICE

Walking with my lover
the nothingness of gray
    over gray-refracted caps
of exhausted waves
    crawling so slowly
        exactly like grief.

At the edge
of receding waters
    walking deeper
    over wet sand
saying a prayer for spirit
        as the flat water
    finally laps my ankles.

Walking with my lover
mellow in part
      limping,
    torn tendons
his asking me
    to tell him something new
    (like a leaf suddenly lifted
    in the wind, or a feather
      spiraling upwards)

even as we walk
toward a friend's house
    locked again,
we have tried before.

XXIX

ALL THE UNRAVELINGS

The needs we each speak
from some larger longing
gather the way light gathers
on leaves yellow-filled

in the fall. Though we meet
like mist breathing
from the trees on the horizon,
we still utter these petitions:

everywhere the sky
has always touched exact—
some answers to need
break almost

full as an egg. You want
to be there, alone, yet here
with hearts' stores.
What shall we say?

Leaves lift
continually toward light.
We touch, almost gilded,
in each unraveling.

xxxii

UNDERNEATH ALL THE FABRICATIONS

for Jim

Here, now, I write to witness
            to one other,
another friend
whose valve in his heart

                    recently replaced
can stretch and restring

exactly like a new aspen leaf
pulled but rebounding
            in spring's first wind

                    —with these words
                    full of milk and stars
                    of grass and birds
of air
and prayer

that maybe,
            despite the odd valve
                    we've opened in our actual
                            atmosphere

maybe,
    despite even our surgical
        strikes,

maybe technology *can* still
    weave
    a new text
    —can be like women of old
    peace-weavers—
    for a living world and words
    where breath is a dance
        rather than fear
    where water is spirit
        rather than poison

I write this with love—
        for the body loves itself
        however politic,

    Loves being
        underneath all the fabrications.

NOTES FROM THE BODY:

If there are things
yet to be said
            and there are
about that which we have said
when not talking

then they must be heard
as notes from my body:

the line from my breast
to my navel your hand
has traced
            sings to your tongue—

the lines around my eyes
            turn to birds' wings
lifting to the sun

when, as on a recent afternoon,
we were done.

It all comes back to the lips,
no longer closed
by things
            said wrongly,

but open to the salt,
open to your breath
            that moves
                  over my body

the way that rain and sun
release from the desert spaces
the most surprising
purple flowers

or—is this more honest?—
like the sounds and songs
we draw,
            each from the other,
that can never be heard
            nor even finally written—

JACQUE VAUGHT BROGAN

is professor of English and American literature at the University of
Notre Dame. She has been the featured poet in several journals, in-
cluding *Connotations,* the *E. E. Cummings Journal,* and *Poetry International.*
Critical works on poetry include *Stevens and Simile: A Theory of Language,
Part of the Climate: American Cubist Poetry, The Violence Within / The Violence
Without: Wallace Stevens and the Emergence of a Revolutionary Poetics,* and *Women
Poets of the Americas: Toward a Pan-American Gathering,* coedited with Cor-
delia Candelaria.